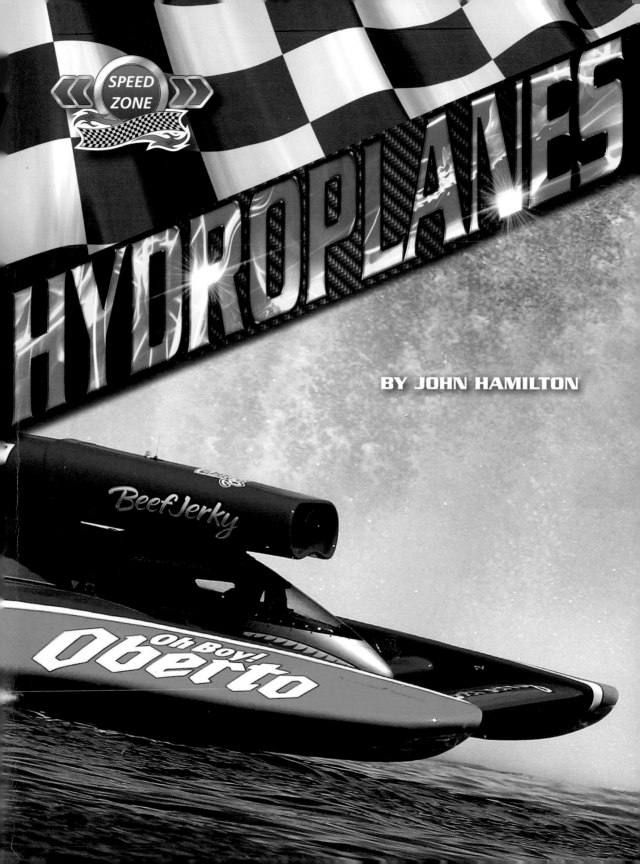

SPEED ZONE

HYDROPLANES

BY JOHN HAMILTON

VISIT US AT WWW.ABDOPUBLISHING.COM

Published by ABDO Publishing Company, PO Box 398166, Minneapolis, MN 55439.
Copyright ©2013 by Abdo Consulting Group, Inc. International copyrights
reserved in all countries. No part of this book may be reproduced in any form
without written permission from the publisher. A&D Xtreme™ is a trademark
and logo of ABDO Publishing Company.

Printed in the United States of America, North Mankato, Minnesota.
052012
092012

Editor: Sue Hamilton
Graphic Design: Sue Hamilton
Cover Design: John Hamilton
Cover Photo: Corbis
Interior Photos: A.K. Bijuraj-pgs 28-29; AP-pgs 6, 7 (bottom) & 8; Corbis-pgs 1 &
20-21; Getty Images-pgs 7 (top) & 22-23; iStockphoto-pg 9 (top & bottom);
Nick Sadowski Photography-pgs 2-3, 4-5, 10-11, 12, 16-17, 18-19, 24-25, 26-27 & 32;
Rommel Bangit-pgs 13 & 14-15; Thinkstock-pgs 1 (Speed Zone graphic) & 30-31.

ABDO Booklinks
Web sites about racing vehicles are featured on our Book Links pages. These links
are routinely monitored and updated to provide the most current information
available. Web site: www.abdopublishing.com

Library of Congress Cataloging-in-Publication Data

Hamilton, John, 1959-
 Hydroplanes / John Hamilton.
   p. cm. -- (Speed zone)
 Includes index.
 ISBN 978-1-61783-528-5
 1. Hydroplanes--Juvenile literature. I. Title.
 VM341.H26 2013
 623.82'314--dc23
                      2012011941

CONTENTS

HYDROPLANES

Hydroplanes are fast race boats. "Hydro" means water. "Plane" is the act of riding a cushion of air near the water's surface. These aerodynamic boats can reach speeds of more than 200 miles per hour (322 kph).

XTREME FACT - Hydroplanes are sometimes called "thunderboats" or "dinoboats" because of the roar from their powerful engines.

5

HISTORY

In the early 1900s, wooden hydroplanes had hulls that looked like a series of steps. During a race, the front of a boat lifted out of the water. It gained speed because there was less friction moving through air than water. Boat designers continued to experiment.

In 1950, boat designer Ted Jones' Slo-mo-shun IV set a world speed record of 160 miles per hour (257 kph).

Slo-mo-shun IV   U-27

By the 1950s, steps were replaced with sponsons. These buoyant chambers on both sides of a boat provide more lift. Wooden hulls were replaced with lightweight fiberglass and other materials.

Driver Donald Campbell broke the world's water speed record in his *Bluebird K7* jet-powered hydroplane in November 1955, reaching 216 mph (348 kph).

By the 1970s, hydroplanes had a distinctive "picklefork" design. Rear wings stabilized the vehicles and powerful helicopter engines blasted the boats across the water.

HYDROPLANE CLASSES

There are many classes of hydroplanes. The smallest use 10-horsepower outboard engines. The largest, most powerful hydroplanes race in the "Unlimited Class." They are between 28 and 32 feet (8.5 and 10 m) long, and weigh a minimum of 6,750 pounds (3,062 kg).

XTREME FACT - The biggest prize in hydroplane racing is the Gold Cup. It was founded in 1904.

Hydroplanes are divided mainly by their weight and the size of their engines. They all race in their own divisions.

PARTS OF A HYDROPLANE

Wing

Engine Cowling

Sponson

Canard

Spar

Propeller

Skid Fin

Rudder

Hydroplanes are made of lightweight aluminum, fiberglass, carbon fiber, and fiber composites. Their design allows them to skim across the water as quickly as possible.

Cockpit

Sponson

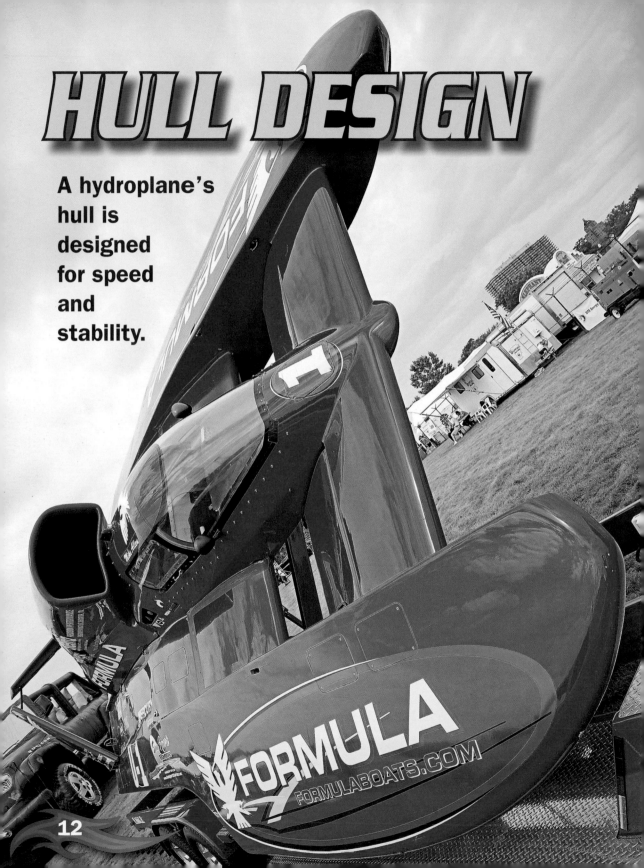

HULL DESIGN

A hydroplane's hull is designed for speed and stability.

XTREME FACT - A popular Unlimited Class hull design is the "picklefork," with sponsons extending forward from the cockpit.

At racing speeds, only three points of a hydroplane actually touch the water: two sponsons (attachments on either side of the hull), plus the bottom half of the propeller. Nicknamed "prop riders," hydroplanes fly like airplanes, but across the surface of the water. They are fast because there is less friction moving through air than water.

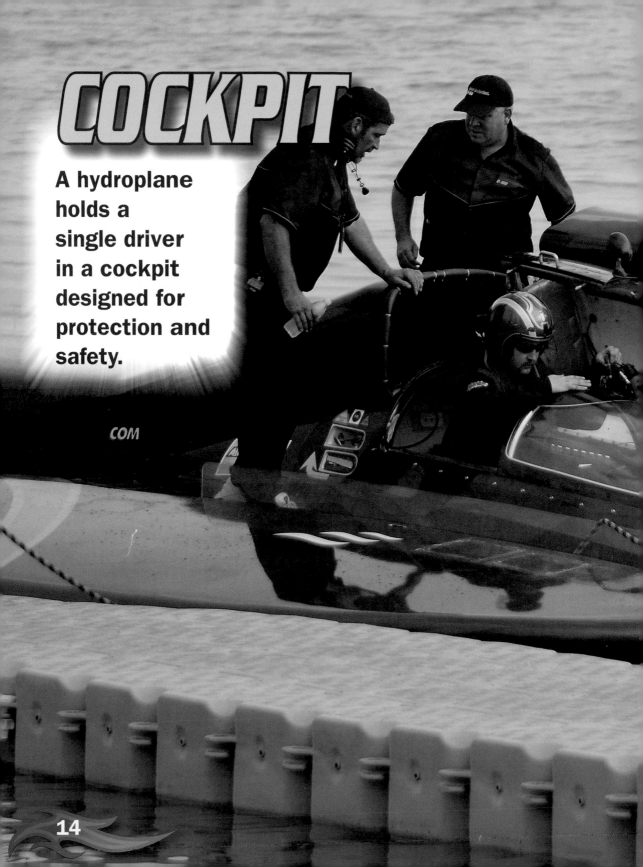

COCKPIT

A hydroplane holds a single driver in a cockpit designed for protection and safety.

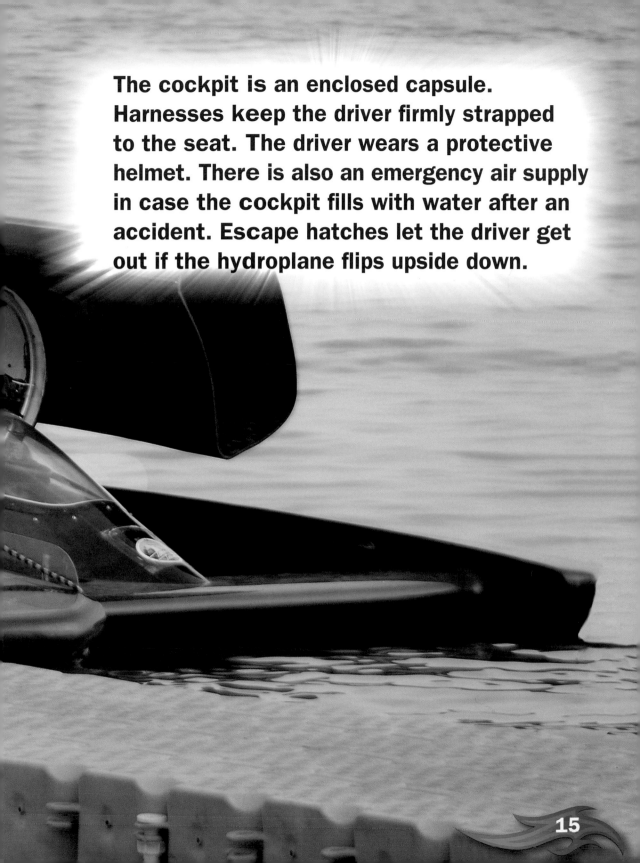

The cockpit is an enclosed capsule. Harnesses keep the driver firmly strapped to the seat. The driver wears a protective helmet. There is also an emergency air supply in case the cockpit fills with water after an accident. Escape hatches let the driver get out if the hydroplane flips upside down.

ENGINE

Today's Unlimited Class hydroplanes use a single Lycoming T-55 L-7 turbine engine, the same kind used to power U.S. Army Chinook helicopters. They run on Jet-A high-quality aviation fuel. There is a large, wide pipe in back that allows heat to escape.

Brian Perkins

OBARZ
FUNERAL HO

XTREME FACT - An Unlimited Class hydroplane engine outputs nearly 3,000 horsepower, the same power as more than 15 average automobiles.

An engine is loaded into an Unlimited Class hydroplane.

PROPELLER

After a race, a hydroplane's propeller sits waiting to be cleaned of weeds.

XTREME FACT - At racing speed, only one of the propeller's three blades touches the water at any given moment.

A hydroplane's powerful engine is connected to a gearbox. Shafts in the bottom of the boat transfer power to the propeller at the rear. Each hydroplane has a single, three-bladed propeller. It is 16 inches (41 cm) in diameter. Propellers can cost more than $15,000 each.

ROOSTER TAILS

When hydroplanes move at racing speed, they create a sheet of water that flies up behind them. These "rooster tails" are created by the boat's propeller and a skid fin that helps keep the boat stable in turns. Rooster tails are dangerous when they obstruct the vision of other drivers.

Two Unlimited Class hydroplanes create rooster tails during a race.

XTREME FACT - The churning propeller blades of Unlimited Class hydroplanes can create rooster tails up to 300 feet (91 m) high.

THE RACE COURSE

The oval-shaped course of a hydroplane race is marked by buoys. Course lengths vary from 1.6 to 2.5 miles (2.6 to 4 km). Races are always run counterclockwise. Drivers must first maintain an average speed of 130 miles per hour (209 kph) in a qualifying lap. Then boats race against each other in several "heats" that usually last three laps. The boats with the most points finally compete against each other in a winner-take-all race.

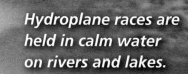
Hydroplane races are held in calm water on rivers and lakes.

HYDROPLANE RACE COURSE

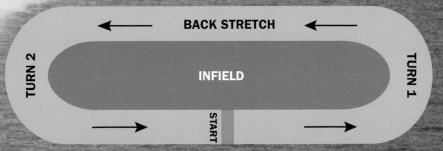

BACK STRETCH ⬅

TURN 2

TURN 1

INFIELD

START

THE FLYING START

To begin a race, hydroplanes take a lap or two to warm up their engines. A one-minute gun goes off, and the racers all fight for the best lane position. As they come down the front straightaway, they stay in their final lanes.

XTREME FACT - The start and finish line is marked with special checkered buoys.

The race begins when a start clock counts down to zero and then begins counting up. Drivers time it so that they cross the starting line just as the clock hits zero. If they cross too soon, they are penalized.

RACING STRATEGY

Speed is important in a hydroplane race, but strategy is equally important. The shortest way around a course is on the inside lanes. However, it is harder to take sharp turns at high speed. Drivers must find the right balance.

Avoiding other boats's rooster tails is also important. For safety reasons, before changing lanes drivers must make sure they are seven boat lengths ahead of any boats behind them. This overlap is about the length of one rooster tail.

DANGERS

With so little of the surface of the boat touching the water, hydroplanes can be very hard to control. Hydroplanes can flip and crash if they take turns too fast, or if they run into the rooster tail of another boat.

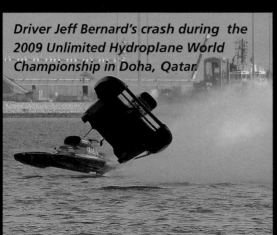

Driver Jeff Bernard's crash during the 2009 Unlimited Hydroplane World Championship in Doha, Qatar.

Fortunately, today's high-tech hydroplanes have many safety features built in that protect the drivers. Still, hydroplane racing is a very dangerous sport.

A "flyover" (or "blowover") happens when a boat goes too fast and gets too much air trapped underneath it. The front part comes up first, and then the boat does an inside-out loop.

Jeff Bernard survived this crash.

GLOSSARY

Aerodynamic

A smooth, streamlined shape that reduces the drag, or resistance, of air moving across its surface. Hydroplanes with aerodynamic shapes go faster because they don't have to push as hard to get through the air.

Canard

A small wing at the front of the boat. Like the rear wing, it helps stabilize the boat, but it can also be adjusted by the driver using foot pedals.

Cowling

A large fiberglass cover. It directs air to the engine and protects against splashing water.

Fiberglass

A reinforced plastic material. Lighter than wood, fiberglass is made of glass fibers embedded in a resin. Many boats today are made with fiberglass.

Horsepower

Horsepower is a unit of measure of power. The term was originally invented to compare the power output of a steam engine with that of an average draft horse.

Hull

The body, or frame, of a boat, including the bottom, sides, and deck.

Picklefork

A hydroplane boat design in which the tips of the two sponsons project forward from the cockpit.

Rudder

A flat piece of metal projecting into the water at the rear of a hydroplane that is used to steer the boat.

Skid Fin

A vertical metal blade that extends below the water line. It is attached to the left sponson. A skid fin helps keep a boat from sliding during a tight turn.

Sponson

An extension on each side of the hull. Sponsons are buoyant chambers that help lift hydroplanes out of the water. At full speed, only the trailing tips of the sponsons, plus the lower half of the propeller, are actually in contact with the water.

Wing

A hydroplane's fixed rear wing is used to stabilize the boat.

INDEX